JNF

This
star
ene

EYEWITNESS
TRAIN

Jigsaw puzzle featuring
Thomas the Tank Engine

Midland Railway coat of arms

Model of 1843 Norris
locomotive

Signal box bell
tapper

Preserved 1938 steam locomotive *Duchess of Hamilton*

EYEWITNESS
TRAIN

WRITTEN BY
JOHN COILEY

Metal whistle

Columbine steam
locomotive, 1845

Railway police
batons

French railways free pass

DUCHESS OF HAMILTON

In association with
THE NATIONAL RAILWAY MUSEUM · YORK

Royal train
headlamp

Passenger
tickets

Station
handbell

REVISED EDITION

DK LONDON

Senior Editor Carron Brown
Designer Chrissy Barnard
Managing Editor Francesca Baines
Managing Art Editor Philip Letsu
Production Editor Robert Dunn
Senior Production Controller Jude Crozier
Senior Jackets Designer Surabhi Wadhwa-Gandhi
Jacket Design Development Manager Sophia MTT
Publisher Andrew Macintyre
Associate Publishing Director Liz Wheeler
Art Director Karen Self
Publishing Director Jonathan Metcalf

Consultant Anthony Coulls

DK DELHI

Senior Editor Priyanka Kharbanda
Senior Art Editor Vikas Chauhan
Art Editors Deepshikha Walia, Aparajita Sen
Picture Researcher Vishal Ghavri
Managing Editor Kingshuk Ghoshal
Managing Art Editor Govind Mittal
DTP Designers Pawan Kumar, Rakesh Kumar, Ashok Kumar
Jacket Designer Juhi Sheth

FIRST EDITION

Project Editor Christine Webb   **Art Editor** Ann Cannings
Managing Editor Helen Parker   **Managing Art Editor** Julia Harris
Production Louise Barratt   **Picture Research** Cynthia Hole
Special Photography Mike Dunning

This Eyewitness ® Book has been conceived by
Dorling Kindersley Limited and Editions Gallimard

This edition published in 2022
First published in Great Britain in 1992 by
Dorling Kindersley Limited
DK, One Embassy Gardens, 8 Viaduct Gardens,
London, SW11 7BW

The authorised representative in the EEA is
Dorling Kindersley Verlag GmbH. Arnulfstr. 124,
80636 Munich, Germany

Copyright © 1992, 2009, 2022 Dorling Kindersley Limited
A Penguin Random House Company
10 9 8 7 6 5 4 3 2 1
001–328180–Aug/2022

A CIP catalogue record for this book is available from the British Library

ISBN: 978-0-2415-5304-6

Printed and bound in China

For the curious
www.dk.com

This book was made with Forest
Stewardship Council™ certified paper –
one small step in DK's commitment to a
sustainable future. For more information
go to www.dk.com/our-green-pledge

MIX
Paper from
responsible sources
FSC™ C018179

Late 19th-century
pocket watch

Mechanical
semaphore signal

Carriage
keys

Model of
American steam
locomotive, 1875

Contents

Sectioned model of 1829 steam locomotive *Novelty*

What is a train?

A train is a series of vehicles on wheels pulled along a railway track by a locomotive. The earliest trains relied on human power to push or pull them along the tracks. Later, horses could pull heavier loads. But it was the invention of the steam locomotive in the early 1800s that led to the rapid rise of the railways. The new powerful steam trains could travel at greater speeds. Steam power lasted until the mid-20th century, when it was replaced by diesel engines and electric motors.

Muscle power

The earliest railways were built in mines to transport coal. To build the longer, public railways, a huge workforce had to dig and move soil, lay tracks, and build bridges and tunnels using basic hand tools and sheer muscle power.

Passenger trains

In the early 1820s and 1830s, carriages in the passenger trains were little more than open wagons with seats (pp. 28-29). Over time, carriages were equipped with lighting, heating, and lavatories. For longer journeys, sleeping and dining cars were available.

Day trippers

Steam trains were a familiar sight by the end of the 19th century. People in rural areas could now travel to the cities for work or pleasure. City dwellers could also enjoy trips to the country or the seaside.

Reproduction 1830 first-class carriage from the Liverpool and Manchester line

LIVERPOOL

HVSKISSON
RAILWAY — COMPANY

Tracks

Electric trains

Electric trains first ran on an underground railway in the 1890s (pp. 56–57). Powered by overhead cables, or from a live rail on the track, electric trains are faster, quieter, and cleaner than diesel or steam locomotives.

Moving goods

The earliest trains were built to move freight (goods) such as coal (pp. 26–27). Today, railways remain an important method of moving freight, although traffic in most countries has declined dramatically due to competition from road transport.

Diesel trains

The first successful passenger diesel trains were introduced in the 1930s in Europe and the USA. Today, diesel power is used worldwide (pp. 40–41).

Locomotive power

The first trains, like this modern reproduction, were hauled by steam locomotives. Nowadays, most trains are hauled by diesel or electric locomotives.

Reproduction of Robert Stephenson's *Rocket* locomotive of 1829

Barrel for water

Tender holds coal and water for the locomotive

The first railways

Railways existed long before steam engines were invented. Heavy loads were transported in wheeled wagons that ran on parallel wooden planks. Later, railways had different guiding systems. Some had rails with flanges to stop the wheels from slipping off. Others had smooth rails, with flanged wheels to keep them on the tracks. Before steam trains, heavy loads were transported by either human power or horsepower.

Ancient roadways

Early civilizations, such as the Babylonians and Sumerians, built roadways made out of stone slabs. As the road surfaces were uneven, grooves were cut into the stone to guide the vehicles. Grooved stone tracks made by the Romans can still be seen in the ruins of Pompeii (above).

Easy rider

Some of the earliest railways in Britain were used to transport coal from the mines to nearby rivers – a journey that was usually downhill. Horses often travelled down in a wagon called a dandy cart to conserve their energy for the long uphill journey back.

This dandy cart was used to transport a horse downhill.

Stagecoach

The stagecoach was the fastest means of transport before the railways. By swapping teams of horses when they tired, stagecoaches and fast mail coaches could travel at an average speed of around 11 kph (7 mph).

Human power

This engraving, published in 1752, was the first illustration of an English railway. It is also the first recorded use of a flanged wheel on a railway in Britain.

Heavy loads

This English railway was built in 1815, and was used for transporting coal. Its rails were made of cast iron. Horses were used to pull the wagons, which were fitted with flanged wheels.

Japanese horsepower

Horse-powered railways were widely used throughout the world until the early 1900s.

Delivering coal

Loaded coal wagons were rolled downhill to nearby rivers. This brakesman controls the wagon's speed using a simple lever brake, while the horse follows behind.

Early German railways

Horses had been used on wagon ways in Germany since the 18th century. The first steam railway in Germany opened in 1835 (see pp. 16–17).

Coal carrier

The wooden wagon used to carry coal in the northeast of England was known as a chaldron. It was loaded from above at the mine. When it arrived at the river, it emptied the coal through a door in the floor directly into the ship waiting below.

A wagon-load of coal became a measure known as a "chaldron".

Brake lever

Flanged wheel

Dawn of the steam age

Ever since the first practical steam engines were designed by Thomas Newcomen in 1712, and James Watt in 1769, engineers tried to use steam power to drive a self-propelled vehicle. It was not until the early 19th century that the first successful steam locomotives were designed. However, engines had to be powerful enough to pull heavy loads, and make as little noise and smoke as possible. They also had to run on smooth rails that would not break under their weight.

Catch Me Who Can

Richard Trevithick built the first working steam locomotive in 1804. It hauled a train of coal wagons and 70 men. This model is based on drawings of his later locomotive *Catch Me Who Can*.

Connecting rods drive the wheel

Beam

Flywheel

Cylinder and piston

Watt's steam engine

In 1769, James Watt invented a steam engine to pump water from mines. Steam pushed a piston to the top of a cylinder. When steam was released, the piston moved down, and the cycle was repeated. The piston was attached to one end of a beam, and its other end turned a wheel called a flywheel. This engine was, however, far too big and heavy for a locomotive.

Local attraction

This engraving shows a steam locomotive built in 1808 by Richard Trevithick. Known as *Catch Me Who Can*, it pulled a four-wheeled carriage round a circular track.

By land and by water
The first self-propelled land vehicle in America was this scow (a type of boat) built by Oliver Evans in 1804. On land, it ran on wheels under its own steam. When it reached water, the wheels were removed.

Getting a grip
For early locomotives, like the one in this 1812 engraving, engineers had to ensure the wheels could grip the smooth rails. They made the driving wheel fit onto a toothed rack running along the rails.

Chaos
This 1828 cartoon shows what the streets of London, UK, might have looked like with the arrival of steam-powered road vehicles.

Puffing Billy is one of the two oldest surviving steam locomotives in the world.

Puffing Billy
Puffing Billy was built by Englishman William Hedley in 1813 and was used to haul coal wagons. Because of complaints about noise and smoke, *Puffing Billy* was adapted so that the steam passed through a "quieting" chamber before going up the chimney.

Coal shovel used on *Puffing Billy*

Fuel supply

The driver stood here.

Steam locomotives come of age

It was the vision of British railway engineer George Stephenson that led the way to the age of steam. Together with his son Robert, Stephenson established his locomotive works in 1823 and began to build steam locomotives for Britain and the world. By the mid-19th century, the steam locomotive had been adopted worldwide as a result of its strength, simplicity, and reliability. The basic principles of the steam locomotive's design remained largely unchanged until diesel-electric and electric locomotives signalled the end of the age of steam.

Best Friend of Charleston
The Best Friend of Charleston was the first successful steam locomotive to be built in the USA. It operated a regular steam passenger service from 1830.

Railway directors were provided with free passes for life, such as this engraved ivory free pass from c. 1830.

Steam for the people
The very first public railway – the Stockton and Darlington Railway – opened in England in 1825. At first, the locomotives on this line were reserved for goods trains. It was not until 1833 that they were used for passenger trains.

Novelty

In 1829, the Rainhill trials were held to choose a locomotive design for the new Liverpool and Manchester Railway in England. One of the entrants, *Novelty*, was a very fast engine, but it broke down too frequently.

Upright boiler

Sectioned model of *Novelty*

American classics

Steam passenger trains were established in the USA by the mid-19th century. US locomotives had large headlamps, wooden "cowcatchers" for sweeping animals off the line, and bronze warning bells.

EYEWITNESS

Putting in a good word

In 1830, British actress Fanny Kemble travelled on *Rocket* from Liverpool to Manchester. Her endorsement helped to make rail travel popular. She wrote, "I closed my eyes and this sensation of flying was quite delightful, and strange beyond description."

Rocket could hit a top speed of

45 kph (28 mph).

Flying Scotsman

By the 1920s, express trains ran throughout the world. One of the most famous, the *Flying Scotsman*, travelled 633 km (392.7 miles) between London and Edinburgh, Scotland.

Chimney expels smoke and steam

Winner takes all

Rocket is one of the most famous locomotives in the world. It entered the 1829 Rainhill trials, and won the competition. British engineer Robert Stephenson was largely responsible for the design of *Rocket*.

Polish stamp showing a locomotive built by Robert Stephenson

How a steam
locomotive works

American steam locomotive

The design of all steam locomotives is based on the same principles. A coal fire in the firebox heats water in the boiler, producing steam. This steam is used to move a piston back and forth. The movement of the piston turns the wheels through a connecting rod and crank system. In all, it takes about three hours for the locomotive to produce enough steam to move.

The boiler contains fire tubes, surrounded by water.

Regulator valve

Superheater tube

Coal burned in firebox

Coupling rod

Crank

The connecting rod drives wheels.

The regulator controls the volume of steam admitted to the cylinders, and so the speed of the locomotive.

The brake lever operates the brake for the locomotive and the train.

The reverser allows the locomotive to be reversed.

Inside the cab

The crew consisted of a driver and a fireman. The driver controlled the locomotive with a regulator, reverser, and brake. The fireman stoked the fire to maintain a constant supply of steam, and ensured there was enough water in the boiler. He also helped the driver to observe signals, especially on curves.

Water tank

Coal space

Front of locomotive

Coal and water are carried in a tender, behind the locomotive.

Two trailing wheels

Six driving wheels

Four leading wheels

Wheel arrangements

Steam locomotives are often described by their wheel arrangements. This locomotive has a 4-6-2 arrangement, with four leading wheels, six driving wheels, and two trailing wheels.

The steam passes through pipes into cylinders.

Chimney

Smokebox

Blast-pipe

The piston valves, sliding back and forth, admit steam to alternate sides of a piston in a power cylinder.

Section of steam locomotive

To make steam, hot gases from the firebox pass through tubes in the boiler and heat the water. The "wet" steam is collected through the regulator valve, then led to the power cylinders. Steam is admitted alternately to either side of a piston in the cylinder, pushing the piston back and forth. The piston is connected to the driving wheels through a connecting rod and crank.

The "to and fro" motion of the piston turns the driving wheel. Each time the cylinder piston moves back and forth, the driving wheel completes a full rotation.

Locomotive has six coupled driving wheels, three of which are seen here

One of three power cylinders in this locomotive

Piston, linked to connecting rod

15

Railways reach the world

The opening of the first "modern" railway in England, in 1830, attracted visitors from all over the world. When other countries began to set up their own railways, many used British designs and equipment for their locomotives, carriages, and track. Later, different countries began to adapt the designs and make their own parts. By the mid-1830s, the USA was exporting steam locomotives to Europe. The railways had a great impact on all aspects of life in many countries, from trade to travel.

Germany's first
The first steam-operated railway in Germany opened in 1835. The English-built locomotive, seen here, was called *Der Adler*.

Headlamp

Indian locomotive
This model shows a typical design of steam locomotive built in Britain for use on the East Indian Railways. Details, such as the sun blinds on the cab windows and the large headlamp, were special adaptations.

Hand rail

Oriental railways
The first steam-worked railway line in Japan opened in 1872. This 19th-century woodblock contrasts modern transport technology of the time – the steam locomotive – with Japan's traditional forms of transport.

Power unit

Hand rail

Parisian steam

This painting shows the first public steam-operated railway in France. Opened in 1837, the line ran from Paris to Le Pecq.

Custom-built

This powerful locomotive was built in Britain in the mid-1930s for use on the Chinese National Railway. The tender is very large as it needed to carry as much water and coal as possible to operate over long distances.

Made in the USA

This is a model of a locomotive built in the USA in 1843. Exported to Austria, it was designed to work on lines with steep slopes and sharp curves.

Travelling home

Built in Britain in 1909 for use in Tasmania, the first Garratt was made of jointed sections, designed for use on lines with sharp curves.

More powerful jointed locomotives (called Beyer-Garratt) of this type were later used in many other countries.

The American railroad

The golden spike
On 10 May 1869, the USA was finally crossed by a railroad from east to west when the last spike, made of gold, joined the Union Pacific Railroad to the Central Pacific Railroad.

A tall chimney improved the draught on the fire and made the locomotive more efficient.

Railways had a huge influence on the history and development of the USA. In Europe, the new railways served existing cities, but in the USA many new towns and cities grew up as a result of the railways. By 1869, people could cross the continent by rail. In the early 20th century, most North Americans lived within 40 km (25 miles) of a railway. Since then, the railways have declined, largely due to competition from road and air transport. But, there has been a renewed interest in the development of electric railways.

Tom Thumb
In 1830, *Tom Thumb*, a small experimental locomotive, made its first run on the Baltimore and Ohio Railroad. It also entered and lost a celebrated race with a horse-drawn train.

Wheel has lip, or flange

It's a first
The *Stourbridge Lion*, the first steam locomotive with flanged wheels to run in the USA, was built in England in 1829. It was similar to the British locomotive *Agenoria* (above).

Driver's cab

Tender

De Witt Clinton

The first steam train in New York State was hauled by the locomotive *De Witt Clinton* in 1831. Passengers rode on top of the vehicles, as well as inside.

Building the future

The opening up of the continent by the spread of railways was a huge achievement. The railways played an important part in the growth, and wealth, of many towns in the USA.

Troublesome times

During the construction of lines westwards from Chicago, trains were sometimes attacked by Indigenous Americans. These were not unprovoked attacks – the local people were trying to defend their way of life, which was being threatened by developers.

Pivoted, or moving, axle

Cowcatcher kept animals from derailing the locomotive.

John Bull

This early locomotive, designed by Robert Stephenson, had a tendency to derail, and became the first locomotive to be fitted with a two-wheeled pivoted axle in front of the driving wheel.

This model is based on an 1875 locomotive that burnt coal.

Typical American locomotive

This model from an 1875 design is typically American, with outside cylinders and a swivelling trolley called a "bogie" in front. The large, ornate cab helps to protect the driver in bad weather. This locomotive burnt coal rather than wood which, until this time, had been used almost universally in the USA.

Steam whistle

Warning bell

Cowcatcher

Bogie

Cowcatcher

Unfenced tracks meant that locomotives could be derailed by animals such as buffalo. The wedge-shaped "cowcatcher" pushed the animal aside. Bells, whistles, and a large headlamp also helped to reduce collisions.

Workman's pick

Building the railways

Far more work goes into building a railway than might be expected. As trains cannot climb very steep hills, they often have to follow longer, less hilly routes. The engineer selects the route by deciding what the steepest slope can be, and considering the type of trains that will use the railway. The route has to be kept as level as possible so builders often make cuttings or tunnels and construct bridges. Steep slopes can be avoided with "S"-shaped bends or spirals.

Hard graft

Early railways were built with basic tools, such as this pick. Other equipment included shovels, shoulder hods (for carrying bricks), barrows, and wooden scaffolding. Gunpowder was used to blast the way through solid rock.

Blood, sweat, and tears

Early cuttings through rock, such as this 1831 example, were excavated with only basic hand tools. A large workforce was needed, and the work took many years to complete.

American construction crew, 1885

The construction crew

In the 19th century, American railways were usually built by crews living in carriages attached to steam locomotives. The train moved the crews along the line as it was completed, as well as providing steam heating and hot water. Earth and rocks removed from cuttings were often used to build embankments.

Building bridges

Before a bridge can be built over a river, builders have to make a temporary island of rocks in the middle, or drive posts into the river bed. This early wooden arch bridge was built on wooden trestles. This design of bridge has been used extensively by the railways.

Model of 1848 wooden arch bridge

Bridges for trains

There are different designs of railway bridge. Cantilever bridges span long distances, for example over water. Arch bridges have a curved support on the section carrying the track. Some bridges, such as the Royal Albert Bridge (right) designed by Isambard Kingdom Brunel in 1859, are based on a mixture of designs.

Illustration of Royal Albert Bridge, near Plymouth, England

Outstanding engineer
Isambard Kingdom Brunel (1806–1859) was appointed the chief engineer for the construction of the Thames Tunnel in London at the age of 19. Considered to be the most innovative engineer of the railway era, he oversaw the construction of the Great Western Railway, as well as designing spectacular bridges and ships.

Coming and going

Passenger stations (pp. 48–49) are designed to help the arrival and departure of passengers and to provide services while they are using the station.

Who pays?

Many railways have been financed by government-issued shares and bonds. This gold bond certificate was issued by the US government to finance railway construction.

Channel tunnel

In 1994, the Channel Tunnel became the first ever rail link between Britain and France (pp. 62–63). The tunnel is 49.8 km (31 miles) long and took six years to build. Tunnel-boring machines worked towards one another from both sides. The machines were later buried as it was too difficult to remove them.

The arch counterbalances the point where the bridge might bend under a heavy load.

Bridges on major rivers had to be high enough so that ships could pass underneath.

Overcoming obstacles

As railway systems grew, engineers had to work out how to overcome obstacles, such as valleys, mountains, lakes, and rivers. Over time, these obstacles were overcome as engineering techniques improved. Tunnels were carved through mountains, and bridges were constructed to span deep valleys and gorges. Powerful locomotives were developed that could climb up steep mountains and go round tight curves Today, there are many high-speed trains on purpose-built lines that can travel over even the most difficult terrain.

Sail by train

Train ferries were introduced in the mid-19th century. Train Ferry 3 (above) carried freight between Harwich and Zeebrugge from 1924 to 1945.

Crossing water

The Firth of Forth bridge in Scotland was opened in 1890. It is the world's oldest railway cantilever bridge (pp. 20–21) and is still in use today.

Tourist attraction

Mountain climbing and sightseeing by steam railway was a great tourist attraction in the 1800s. The Snowdon Mountain Railway opened in Wales in 1896, using a rack and pinion system to climb the steep slopes.

Mount Washington Cog Railway

The world's first mountain rack railway opened in 1869 in New Hampshire, USA. This line originally used a wrought-iron rack, somewhat like a ladder.

Model of Kitson-Meyer type of tank locomotive built in 1903

A.C.N.R

Swivelling power bogie

Staying power

Powerful locomotives were needed in rugged countryside with steep slopes and tight bends. To help these long, heavy machines to go round tight curves, swivelling trolleys with wheels (bogies) were attached underneath the frame carrying the boiler.

Rigi railway

In 1873, a steam-operated railway opened to the top of Mount Rigi in Switzerland using a rack and pinion system. A toothed rack was laid between the rails, and a powered cog on the locomotive drove the train up the mountain.

Sydney Harbour Bridge

The Sydney Harbour Bridge is famous for its characteristic shape on the Sydney skyline. When it opened in 1932, it carried two railway lines and two tram lines. Now it carries trains, eight road lanes, a footpath, and a cycle track.

The cantilever Forth Rail Bridge, Scotland, is a **UNESCO World Heritage Site**.

Making tracks

Rails were used to guide loaded wagons long before the steam locomotive was invented. However, the early cast-iron rails were not strong enough to carry heavy steam locomotives. Cast-iron rails were replaced by stronger, wrought-iron rails until the 1870s, when steel tracks were introduced. Tracks are constantly being improved to carry heavier, faster trains. For a smoother ride, most main lines have continuously welded rails, instead of jointed short lengths. The distance between the rails is known as the gauge.

Track marks

The track layout at the approach to busy stations can be extremely complex. To enable trains to switch lines, special points (where trains change direction) were installed.

Laying tracks

Building early railways required large groups of people working together to lift and position rails.

Flanged plateway to keep wheels on

Lines merge at points

Section of early plateway, 1799

Plateway

Wagons often had to be moved from one line to another. This was done by merging two lines at points, or switches. Flanged plateways (above) were replaced in the 1820s by smooth edge rails, for wagons with flanged wheels (with a lip on them).

Bull-head rail, 1870

Rail sections

Railway engineers tried many rail designs before they came up with the flat-bottomed rail. These rail sections are some of the early designs.

"Head" of rail

This type of rail has been used in Britain since the 1850s.

Saddleback or Barlow rail, used from 1849

Flat-bottomed rail, 1884

Plate rail

Early rails, such as this plate rail from 1808, were made of cast iron in short sections, and supported by stone sleepers.

Outside flange to guide wheels without a flange

Dangerous times

Railway dramas often featured in early films. Here the heroine is being tied to a track of flat-bottomed rails.

Wooden "key"

Screw fastens chair to sleeper.

Cast-iron chair

Bull-head rail

This section of steel bull-head rail is secured in a cast-iron chair by a wooden "key". The chair is secured to a wooden sleeper by large screws.

Making changes

Problems arose where railways with different gauges met. Changing trains was particularly difficult for passengers with a lot of luggage.

Flat-bottomed rail

Modern flat-bottomed rails are made of steel. The rails are secured on a rubber pad, which is fastened to a concrete sleeper by a steel spring.

Head of steel rail

Steel spring secures rail to sleeper.

Sleeper supports the track and keeps the gauge correct.

Fish-belly rails

These cast-iron rails were designed for strength. A deeper section, halfway along the rail, was designed to resist heavy weights.

Flanged wheel fits over plain edge rail.

F.D. BANISTER Esq, C.E.

Gauge measure

Special steel rails were used to check the gauge (distance) between rails. The gauge was measured from the inside edge of one rail to the inside edge of the other. The standard gauge in Britain, and most of Europe and North America, is 1,435 mm (4 ft 8.5 in).

Freight trains

The earliest trains were freight trains that carried goods such as coal. At first, these trains consisted of two or three simple wagons hauled by a horse. However, with the development of the steam locomotive (pp. 10–11) trains became much longer and faster, making rail freight more efficient. In the early days, all freight trains were very slow because their basic brake systems could not stop trains fast enough in an emergency. Technical developments since then now mean that freight trains can run at higher speeds.

Go by rail
This East German stamp shows how moving heavy goods by rail helps to reduce road congestion.

Shedding the load
Modern freight trains carry goods in huge, standard-sized containers (pp. 62–63). These can be stacked and moved from train to ship, truck, or aircraft without unpacking. Previously, cranes had to unload hundreds of different-sized containers.

Brake van
Most freight trains ran with wagons that were not connected to brakes. The only means of controlling the train was to apply the brake on the locomotive and the guard's hand brake on the "brake" van. This meant that freight trains could travel no faster than 50 kph (30 mph).

Milk tanker
The new railways meant that milk and fish could be delivered speedily from rural areas to the cities. By the 1930s, milk was transported in special glass-lined tankers.

Shunter's pole with metal hook

Safety first
For many years, wagons were joined by three chain links. It was the shunter's job to couple (join) and uncouple the wagons. To avoid the risk of being injured between the wagons, shunters used a long pole with a metal hook.

Taillight

All trains carry a red tail lamp. This modern electric battery version gives a flashing signal.

By the mid-1950s, most freight trains in the USA were hauled by diesel engines.

Bulk loads

Most freight trains now haul bulky loads in purpose-built wagons, fitted with driver-operated brakes. This means that they can run safely at more than 100 kph (60 mph), like this one near Montana, USA.

Coal wagon from the Stanton coal mine in the north of England

Coal wagon

For many years, coal was carried in Britain in simple wagons owned by individual coal mines. The wagons were usually loaded automatically from above, but they often had to be unloaded by workers with shovels.

American first-class ticket

Australian second-class ticket

British third-class ticket

Paying the way
These tickets are similar to the first card tickets that were made in 1837.

First, second, and third class

The first public passenger trains were very different from today's comfortable, spacious trains. They offered three different classes of accommodation. The enclosed first-class compartment had glass windows and padded seats. The second class was an open wagon with seats, while there were no seats in the third class. Over the years, trains were equipped with heating, lighting, and corridors that provided access to lavatories and to restaurant cars.

Early days
Early images of passenger trains from the 1830s show the first-class carriages carrying luggage – and guards – on the roof. Second- and third-class vehicles were not enclosed.

A fresh start
The development of railways and steamships in the 19th century led to large-scale immigration, particularly from Europe to North America. After crossing the Atlantic, immigrants travelled westwards on very crowded trains.

Private rooms
First-class passengers travelled in spacious carriages, and they were even able to hold private conversations.

Third-class compartment

Lavatory

WATERLOO

THIRD   6474   FIRST   LSWR

First class

First-class travellers had comfortable seats and the most legroom. Passengers in this compartment had the smoothest journey, as they were farthest from the bumps and jolts of the wheels.

Second class

Compared with first class, this compartment was simpler and had less legroom. Second-class compartments were phased out from British trains soon after this carriage was built.

Hard times

In the early days, third-class travel was a far cry from first class. Three or four times as many passengers were crowded into the same space.

Third class

This compartment was the simplest and had the least room. However, it was far better than the cramped conditions of the earliest third-class compartments. Located over the wheels, its occupants had a bumpy, noisy ride.

Carriage keys

Carriages were locked when not in use. The lock is operated by a square-shaped key.

Three-in-one

This 1904 carriage (below) is unusual in having first-, second-, and third-class accommodation in the same vehicle, with no connecting corridor. Each compartment had access to a lavatory.

First-class compartment

Second-class compartment

SECOND   6474

Gold pass allowing senior railway staff free first-class travel

Travelling in style

American Pullman train pass

French free pass

American free pass for Atchison, Topeka & Santa Fe railway

By the 1850s, the railways of Europe and the USA were offering first-class passengers luxurious facilities including heating, lighting, toilets, and catering. In the USA, businessman George Pullman introduced the first luxury sleeping cars in 1865, then first-class dining facilities. Soon afterwards, railway companies with long-distance passenger services started to build hotels alongside their main stations. From then on, travelling by rail became a stylish affair for those who could afford it.

China and roses

Trains with first-class dining cars would serve meals on fine china table settings. This breakfast setting was made in the 1930s and has a delicate gilt border with pink roses.

Top-notch travellers

People such as railway directors who held free passes were able to travel first class all over the world.

Travel a la mode

Striking images of elegant travellers from the 1920s and 1930s are sometimes still used by companies to promote their trains.

Exclusive eating

Dining in a first-class restaurant car was just as enjoyable as dining in an exclusive restaurant – with the added bonus of a constantly changing view.

Anyone for cocktails?

In the 1930s, even cocktails could be ordered by first-class passengers in Britain. Each railway company had their own monogram, which decorated glasses, silverware, and china.

Whodunnit?

Famous luxury trains have been the setting for many novels and films, including Agatha Christie's *Murder on the Orient Express* (1934).

1960

Symbol of luxury

The British Pullman Company coat of arms appeared on the exterior of all its carriages. Pullman cars operated in Britain from 1874 until the 1980s.

Detailed marquetry (inlay) on wood-panelled walls

Bellpush for calling attendant

Pullman style

The interior of the 1914 Pullman car *Topaz* (left and below) was the ultimate in comfort. British-built Pullman cars were known for their magnificent detailed woodwork. Every armchair had a glass-topped table in front of it, together with a brass lamp and a bellpush for calling the attendant. At each end of this car were private compartments for four, known as coupés.

Pullman comfort

By the 1870s, American Pullman cars provided all that was needed for a long-distance journey. Travellers could even join in the Sunday hymns.

Oval lavatory window

Brass handrails

In the signal box

The signal box plays an important role in railway safety. In the early days, people waved flags or batons to signal when trains could move. If a train had to change direction at a junction, the "points" were operated manually to switch the train to the right track. The invention of the electric telegraph in the 1850s enabled signalmen to send an electric bell code down the line. This development led to each train being separated by a section of railway, called a "block". The signals and points for each "block" were controlled mechanically from the signal box.

The signal box had an oil lamp in case of power failure.

On the platform

In France, the levers for signals and points were often placed behind barriers on the platform. This allowed the signalman to perform other duties between signalling trains.

Bell sounds coded message from signal boxes on either side of this one.

Yellow lever operates a distant (warning) signal.

Two red levers for stop signals pulled into "off" or "clear" position

Blue levers control locks on points, black levers control points, and white levers are spare.

What's what?

This signal box has 40 levers for operating the signals and points. Above it are electrical instruments to send and receive signals. Other instruments, called block instruments, indicate whether the line is empty, or occupied by a train. There are also "locks" between the instruments, signals, and the track. These ensure that trains are correctly signalled, and that a train cannot be overlooked if it has broken down.

Single line
electric
key token
instrument

*Staffs for
a journey in
the opposite
direction were
locked into
the key token
until the line
was clear.*

EYEWITNESS

A helping hand

When signalman James Wide lost both his legs in a railway accident in South Africa, he trained his pet baboon Jack to operate the railway signals under supervision. From 1881 to 1890, Jack carried out his job with no errors.

Three-position block instrument

This instrument indicated to the signalman the state of the line between his box and the one before.

Bell tapper

To ask if the line was clear, the signalman used a bell tapper to send bell codes to the boxes on either side of him.

All clear

To operate the points and signals, the signalman had to pull the long levers that were linked to the points by rods, and to the signals by cables.

Extra protection

Trains that travelled both ways on single lines depended on key token instruments. A signal could be given to the driver only once he had been handed a metal staff, coded for the journey.

Three-position pegging block instrument

This instrument sent information to the three-position block instrument. It also displayed the state of the line.

Modern signal box

In the early 1900s, signal boxes were manually operated. A modern signalling control centre is programmed to run automatically unless there is a problem, such as a failed train, derailment, or broken signal. Then the signaller can set alternative routes to deal with the problem.

Following the signs

The first train drivers relied on hand signals given by railway policemen to avoid collisions with other trains. Later, mechanical signals were introduced. As train speeds rose, more sophisticated equipment was needed to improve rail safety. By the 1920s, railways were equipped with electric colour light signals that were more powerful and easier to see at a distance, especially at night. All high-speed main lines now use colour light signals that, along with the points on the track, are indicated automatically in the signal box.

Stop the train!
At small rural stations in Australia, passengers stopped the train by waving a tin flag.

The red, square-ended arm is horizontal, meaning "stop".

Signalman's badge

Identification
Most people working on the railways wore identification badges as part of their uniform.

Signalling oil lamp
In the past, the guard would signal to the driver at a station using a flag. At night, an oil lamp was used. The glass in this lamp was rotated to give a green (go), red (stop), or white (general) signal.

Three-aspect guard's lamp

Mechanical semaphore signal
The upper arm of this mechanical signal indicates whether or not a train should stop. The lower arm serves as a distant (warning) signal. It tells the driver to prepare to stop at the next signal. Here both signals are horizontal and indicate "stop".

Truncheons and armband
Early railway policemen used different coloured flags to signal that the line was clear, or that a train must stop or proceed with caution. The railway police wore armbands for identification and carried ornate truncheons in case of trouble.

Armband and truncheons

The road barrier comes down across the road when a train is due.

Dwarf semaphore signal

Small "dwarf" signal arms were used for shunting trains. This example is operated by a combination of electricity and a pneumatically operated arm.

All clear

When both signals are raised, this means that the line ahead is clear. The driver may proceed at normal speed.

Level crossing

Most road and railway intersections in the USA have no road barriers. They are protected by flashing lights and a ringing bell.

Train approaching

In the early 20th century, when drivers approached a large junction station, they were faced with a complicated array of signals and tracks.

Proceed with caution

The "stop" signal is raised but the "distant" (warning) signal remains horizontal. This means that the driver may proceed with caution, but must be prepared to stop at the next red signal.

The yellow "warning" arm is raised, meaning "all clear".

The yellow "distant" warning arm is horizontal, meaning "proceed with caution".

Rail safety pioneer

William Hunter Dammond (1873–1956) was an American civil engineer who was a pioneer in rail safety. He took his ideas for track circuiting to the UK, including replacing hand signallers with technology to reduce human error. His ideas were not widely taken up at the time, but later led to improvements.

Modern lights

Signals that use LEDs (Light Emitting Diodes) are brighter and need less maintenance than signals with conventional bulbs. Railways all over the world now use LED signals.

Post haste

The travelling post office van was designed to handle all the jobs carried out in a normal post office – while the train sped along. Without stopping, the van could pick up mail from specially designed equipment beside the track. The mail was then sorted and put into sacks to be dropped off along the route. The equipment for collecting and dropping off the mail was located at one end of the vehicle. The rest of the van held sorting tables, pigeon-holes, and sacks for sorted mail.

American mail

This American locomotive from the 1870s is hauling a mail train. Mailbags are thrown down for collection, while similar bags to be picked up hang from a post.

Mail to be collected by train

Postbox for late letters. Letters posted here carried an extra fee.

Pigeon-holes for sorting letters

The apparatus for exchanging mail bags from a moving train was last used in 1971.

Net collects mail pouch from arm lowered from train.

Leather bag with sorted mail to be dropped off

What goes where?

Incoming mail was emptied onto the sorting table, and individual letters were put into pigeon-holes. When there were enough letters for one destination, they were bundled up and put in a sack. The sacks were dropped off along the route.

Post by rail

The strong association between trains and mail is illustrated by this 1974 Liberian postage stamp.

Swiftly by post

The "Irish Mail" ran between London and Holyhead from 1848 until 2002. As well as mail, the train also carried passengers, and offered sleeping accommodation.

Post office on wheels

In 1838, it was decided that the Royal Mail should be carried by rail, rather than by mail coaches. In the USA, the first purpose-built railway Post Office car ran in 1864. The railways are still used today by mail services around the world.

Net picks up mail bag.

W G J S
N 21 9 G

Travelling Post Office van, 1885

Picking up

This cigarette card shows a Travelling Post Office train picking up local mail at speed.

Trackside equipment

Mail to be picked up was suspended beside the track in a pouch, which was swept into a net put out from the van just before the collection point. Mail to be dropped off hung from an arm that swung out just before the train reached the collecting net.

Road to rail

This British mail van is delivering mail to a local train station. The mail was taken to a mainline station, before being put aboard a Travelling Post Office Train (TPO). The last TPO ran in Britain in 2004.

Electric trains

Engineers developed the first electric trains towards the end of the 19th century. Some locomotives collected power from overhead cables, while others took power from a third "live" rail on the track. Electric locomotives have many advantages over steam and diesel power. They are faster, quieter, and easier to run. Although building an electric railway or electrifying an existing one is expensive, electric trains are both economic and efficient, and are now widely used on underground and commuter services around the world.

American first
The first electric locomotives on an American main line were introduced on the Baltimore and Ohio Railroad in 1895. This route passed through many tunnels, which had filled with choking fumes during the days of steam.

Early electric locomotive
This electric locomotive was built to replace steam locomotives on a freight line. The locomotive was designed to collect the electric current either by overhead pantograph or from a third "live" rail.

The pantograph, or the "arm", on top collects current from the overhead power line.

This electric locomotive was built in 1904 by the North Eastern Railway, England.

NORTH   EASTERN

Swift and safe

The French railways used striking posters to advertise their new electric services in the early 1900s. This poster promoted the fast, clean electric trains running from Paris to Versailles.

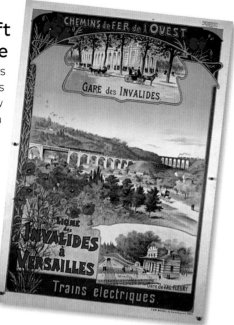

Werner von Siemens
German engineer Werner von Siemens (1816–1892) made his name at an exhibition in Berlin, Germany, in 1879. He showcased the first practical electric passenger train. By doing so, he laid the future for the world's railways for almost a century.

Le Mistral

This classic French train was hauled by a powerful electric locomotive. It was famed for its comfortable high-speed service between Paris and Nice.

Changing designs

The latest designs of electric trains always run the risk of being overshadowed by better, more advanced designs. The fastest electric locomotives in the UK are the Class 91, but the Hitachi 800 series trains – the Azuma – used on the electrified main line between London and Edinburgh in Scotland can accelerate and slow down much more quickly, allowing them to reduce the journey time by as much as 18 minutes.

The first practical electric railway was designed by German engineer **Werner von Siemens in 1879**.

Very, very fast

The world speed record for a passenger train was achieved by France's TGV (Train à Grande Vitesse) in 2007 when it reached 574.8 kph (357 mph). The orange TGV, introduced in 1981, was in operation until 2020. It was made up of eight carriages with an electric locomotive at either end.

Diesel power

The invention of the diesel-powered locomotive, along with the electric locomotive, signalled that the age of steam was drawing to a close. The diesel engine was first demonstrated in 1893 by German engineer Dr Rudolph Diesel, who went on to build the world's first reliable diesel engine in 1897. In most diesel locomotives, the engine powers a generator that produces an electric current. This drives the locomotive's electric motors, which turn the wheels.

Plastic top protects from grease and dirt.

Driver's cap

Steam-engine drivers wore special caps to signify their position. The caps were also useful for keeping soot and coal dust out of the hair.

Fan cools generator

The diesel engine

In a diesel engine, heavy diesel oil is injected into a cylinder of hot air. The fuel ignites, and the energy released drives the generator. The generator makes electricity, which drives a motor that turns the wheels.

Generator produces an electric current, which is used to drive the wheels

Diesel engine drives generator

DELTIC

Snack time

Train drivers often had a snack and hot drink along the way. The lunch box and mash can here are from the days of steam.

Mash can for hot drinks

Time saver

High-speed diesel-electric trains are designed to save time and labour. Instead of the traditional set of carriages hauled by a locomotive, the carriages travel between two diesel-electric power cars. At the end of the journey, the locomotive does not have to be replaced.

High-speed diesel

One of the first successful high-speed diesel trains was the American *Zephyr*. In 1936, it achieved an average speed of 134 kph (83.3 mph) over the 1,609-km (1,000-mile) route from Chicago to Denver.

Trans-Europ-Express

The Trans-Europ-Express was a fast, luxurious service, designed to transport businesspeople between major European cities. The diesel-electric trains on these lines only catered for first-class passengers.

Prototype British Rail *Deltic* diesel-electric locomotive, 1955

Prototype locomotive

When this Deltic diesel-electric locomotive was built in 1955, it was the most powerful diesel-electric single-unit locomotive in the world. In 1961, the Deltics replaced the powerful steam locomotives on the East Coast main line between London and Edinburgh (pp. 46–47). In the 20 years that they worked this line, they each ran more than 4.8 million km (3 million miles).

East German stamp featuring a diesel locomotive for shunting and local freight services

20 DDR

Schienenfahrzeuge aus der DDR

DIESELLOKOMOTIVE BR 110   1979

Long distance by train

Early journeys on long-distance railways were often slow and uncomfortable. Over time, the facilities on long-distance trains improved with the introduction of heating, lighting, and special carriages for sleeping and dining. Today, most business people fly on longer journeys to save time. Long-distance trains, however, still remain popular with tourists. For those who are not in a hurry, travelling by train is an excellent way to see a country's landscape and scenery.

Straight and narrow
The first through service from Sydney on the east coast of Australia to Perth on the west coast was introduced in 1970. The luxury *Indian Pacific* train covers the 4,352-km- (2,704-mile-) route in four days.

Containers for tea and coffee

Saucepan

Snack time
Many passengers on long-distance journeys brought their own refreshments in luncheon baskets, such as this one containing tea-making equipment. Self-catering on trains remained popular even after the introduction of restaurant cars in 1879.

Wagons-Lits car
The Wagons-Lits Company, founded in 1876, operated high-quality sleeping and dining cars across Europe.

Blue Train
A luxury train has run between Cape Town and Pretoria in South Africa since 1903. In 1939, the *Blue Train* was introduced on this 1,540-km (956-mile) stretch, and it is now regarded as one of the most luxurious trains in the world.

Trans-Siberian railway

A passenger train between Moscow and Vladivostock makes one of the longest regular train journeys in the world. It takes eight days to travel 9,297 km (5,778 miles).

Sleeping car

Passengers could travel in comfortable sleeping cars from the 1860s in the USA, and from the 1870s in Europe. This two-berth compartment on a 1936 Wagons-Lits sleeping car travelled overnight between London, Paris, and Brussels. During the day, the lower berth was converted into seats. Trains on this route crossed the Channel on board a train ferry.

Train ferry

The Dover–Dunkerque train ferry, linking England with France, came into service in 1936. The ferry ceased running in 1995 and all freight traffic now goes by lorry or via the Channel Tunnel.

Super Chief ticket of 1938

Super service

The American *Super Chief* service ran between Los Angeles and Chicago. Known for its fine dining, it established a reputation as the best long-distance train in the USA.

Royal trains

Some of the most splendid railway carriages ever built were constructed for the British Royal Family. Since the first royal railway journey in 1839, the Royal Family have travelled by train when making longer journeys around Britain. The railways offered greater comfort, space, and privacy than road transport. When built, the royal carriages represented the latest in design and technology. Royal trains are still used today.

Royal regalia

Locomotives that were used to haul royal trains, like *Gladstone* (above and below), usually carried elaborate cast-metal coats of arms and flags.

Gladstone's lamp

Oil headlamps on royal locomotives were often decorated, such as this one from *Gladstone*.

Attendants' compartment

Royal stations

Some stations were built especially for royal use, such as this one at Gosport, which Queen Victoria used when travelling to her residence on the Isle of Wight. The station was richly decorated for her arrival.

By day, the Queen sat in the coupé compartment, which had end windows.

№ 2

Queen's carriage

The first royal saloon was made for the Dowager Queen Adelaide in 1842 (right). The design was based on three stagecoach compartments, with a beautifully furnished and upholstered interior. It is thought that the Queen travelled during the day in the end (or coupé) compartment, with close attendants in the middle compartment.

The footrail and the step above allowed access from ground level.

Queen Victoria's day saloon

No expense was spared in the decoration of the day saloon, which was chosen by Queen Victoria. The wood was maple, the upholstery was blue watered silk, and the ceilings were covered in white quilted silk. The saloon was originally lit with oil lamps, but in 1895 newly developed electric lighting and bells for calling attendants were added.

Stretching out

At night, the Queen would transfer to the compartment at the other end, where the cushions were rearranged into a bed. The boxlike extension at the end provided extra room for feet and legs.

Sleeping compartment

"Boot", or boxlike, extension

Wooden chassis (framework) with four wheels

Queen Victoria's lavatory

This toilet and washing compartment was beautifully furnished in maple and blue silk.

King Edward VII's smoking compartment

The King's wood-panelled compartment of 1902 contained fans, heaters, and even cigar-lighters.

Queen Alexandra's bedroom

The Queen could use the buttons above her bed to summon her servants during the night.

Queen Mary's day compartment

The saloon contained a day compartment, together with a dressing room, bathroom, and bedroom.

Record breakers

From the earliest days of steam to the present day, speed records have been, and are still being, set and broken. For Britain and the USA, breaking the speed barrier of one hundred miles per hour was a special target. This target was supposedly met in 1893, when an American locomotive was claimed to have reached a speed of 181 kph (112.5 mph), and in 1904, when a British locomotive was timed at 164 kph (102 mph). However, serious doubts were later cast on both these claims.

Fast movers

The first steam engines designed to run at 161 kph (100 mph) on every trip operated the 1935 *Hiawatha* service between Chicago and Minneapolis/ St Paul in the USA. The service holds the record for the fastest steam-powered run between two stations on a scheduled service.

The best ever

The brass plaque on the boiler of *Mallard* commemorates the world speed record for a steam locomotive set on 3 July 1938.

ON 3RD JULY 1938 THIS LOCOMOTIVE ATTAINED A WORLD SPEED RECORD FOR STEAM TRACTION OF 126 MILES PER HOUR

Steam train of the *Hiawatha* service

Like a bullet

When opened in 1964, the Japanese electric Shinkansen, or "bullet train" between Tokyo and Osaka was the first of a new generation of high-speed railways built exclusively for intercity passenger trains.

The Journey Shrinker

In 1985, the British Rail High Speed Train (HST) reached a record speed for a diesel locomotive of 232 kph (144 mph), earning it the name "The Journey Shrinker".

The fastest ever

The TGV *(Train à Grande Vitesse)*, a French electric high-speed train, was introduced in 1981 between Paris and Lyon. TGVs run on specially designed tracks, and travel up to 320 kph (200 mph). In 2007, a modified TGV achieved a world record of 574.8 kph (357 mph) on the Paris to Strasbourg line.

Steam record

The steam locomotive *Mallard* was designed by British engineer Sir Nigel Gresley. In July 1938, *Mallard* set a world speed record for a steam locomotive of 203 kph (126 mph). It was pulling a special train on the main line between London and Edinburgh. This record still stands.

Mallard was built by the London North Eastern Railway in 1938.

At the station

The very first stations were simple wooden shelters built next to the rail track. Today, some small rural stations are still very simple buildings, providing little more than a ticket counter and a waiting room. But in many major towns and cities, railway stations are busy transport hubs, offering a wide range of shops, cafes, refreshment rooms, and car parks. Often, the station is one of the largest buildings in town, with imposing architecture in styles from all ages from classical to ultra-modern.

A large clock is often the focal point of a station.

Country station

Simple stations in rural areas often had a very low platform, or none at all. Passengers entered or left the train by climbing onto steps on the carriages.

Time in hand

To keep trains to a strict timetable, stations had large clocks, while railway staff carried pocket watches.

Late 19th-century pocket watch

MS&LRY

Handbell

Before electricity was available to operate electric bells, handbells were rung to announce the arrival of a train.

LC & DR
N & SW

London, Chatham, and Dover Railway insignia

Railway time

In the early days, trains that ran east to west in large countries such as the USA experienced problems with timekeeping. Eventually, these countries were divided into different time zones, so the time changed whenever a train crossed into a new zone.

JOHN WALKER
1. SOUTH MOLTON ST.
LONDON
1130

Waterloo station

Large stations, such as this one, are designed so that huge numbers of passengers can quickly board or leave their train during peak hours.

Tickets please!

Tickets were proof that passengers had paid the fare. A ticket inspector marked the ticket with a clipper so that it could not be used again. Modern digital tickets usually have a QR code or bar code that can be scanned at the station or on the train.

Japanese railway tickets

QR code

An electronic train ticket

A first-class ticket to Basra in Iraq

Clipper

Special delivery

In the 1920s and 1930s, the railways ferried freight to and from stations using their own road vehicles. Bicycles were used for delivering small, local parcels.

SOUTHERN RAILWAY PARCEL DELIVERY SERVICE FROM HORSTED KEYNES STATION

Simple metal whistle

Whistle stop

Simple whistles made from wood or metal were used by platform staff to let the driver know when a train was ready to depart.

Railway uniform button forms part of this whistle.

The romance of steam

The days of steam are often portrayed as a romantic age. The classic film *Brief Encounter* (1945) is based on a chance meeting at a railway station shortly after World War II.

Landmark station

With their imposing architecture, stations such as the Gare de Lyon in Paris became familiar landmarks.

Grand Central Station

New York's Grand Central Station is the largest railway station in the world. Information boards on its huge concourse show where and when the trains are arriving and departing.

Running the railway

British porter's cap badge

Oiling the wheels

Steam train drivers were responsible for checking their trains were in working order.

Many people are required for the smooth running of a railway. The commercial departments specify the type, frequency, and speed of trains needed. The operating department meets these demands. The technical engineering department provides the equipment, while the civil engineering team ensures that the track and fixed structures are functional. All this work is supported by many other departments.

Russian railway worker's badge

Chinese railway worker's badge

Great Western Railway fireman's helmet

Smooth operation

As railway companies needed a wide variety of workers to run smoothly, they were traditionally among the world's largest employers.

Waiter
Chef
Engine driver
Shunter
Signalman
Fireman
Ticket inspector
Porter
Station-master
Guard

Safety first

The railways ran their own fire service, trained to deal with any special hazards. The service had its own equipment and uniform.

Travellers' helper

In the past, railway companies owned many of the station hotels. The hotel porter assisted passengers entering and leaving the hotel.

Station-master

The station-master was in charge of all aspects of running the station and ensured that trains arrived and departed promptly.

The permanent way

A great deal of organization went into maintaining the track. The look-out man, in charge of the working team, would blow a horn to warn of an approaching train.

The railway track was known as "the permanent way".

Indispensable

Even with today's new equipment, the signal engineer still plays a vital role. However, all modern signal equipment is designed to be "fail-safe" by showing red stop signals in case of malfunction.

Topping up

While at the station, a long-distance train had to be stocked up with enough food and water to last until the next refuelling stop. This water carrier was used to top up the dining car's tank with drinking water. The tanks for the lavatories were refilled with hoses linked to local water supplies.

The hose is fitted into the dining car's water tank.

When the wheel turns, it pumps water through the hose.

Oilcan from around 1890

Useful tool

This oilcan was used for filling oil lamps. The broad base makes it difficult to knock over.

The water carrier is wheeled along the platform.

Thick, multi-stranded wick

Lighting up

Flare lamps provided light before electric battery lamps came along. The oil in the lamp was burned at the end of the wick. The lamp warned of hazards in yards, as well as being used for inspecting steam locomotives.

Oil flare lamp from around 1900

Still in steam

In most parts of the world, steam locomotives are a thing of the past. Cleaner, more efficient diesel and electric trains have taken their place. However, there is still considerable interest in steam engines among rail enthusiasts. Some modern, more efficient, steam locomotives are still used on tourist lines in countries such as Switzerland. Hundreds of preserved steam locomotives are owned by railway societies and transport museums across the world, and many have been carefully restored to working order. They are used to pull trains on preserved lines, or on the quieter scenic lines of national railway networks.

New locomotives

Completed in 2008, *Tornado* was the first main line steam locomotive to be made in the UK since 1960. It has run all over the UK in the years since and reached a milestone speed of 161 kph (100 mph) in 2017.

Keeping on track

Steam trains were used in India until the end of the 20th century. Narrow gauge locomotives, such as this one, were imported to India from France, Germany, and Japan.

In 1958, British Railways had
16,000 steam locomotives,
but by the end of 1968, there were none.

Star exhibit

Evening Star was the last steam locomotive built for British Rail in 1960. It was originally intended for freight work, but it also pulled passenger and express trains until 1966. It is now displayed in Britain's National Railway Museum.

Tourist attractions

Many steam railways are now tourist attractions. The first was the Talyllyn Railway in Wales, saved in 1951 and run by volunteers in their spare time. Across the world, new steam locomotives have been built to reproduce old designs or to operate specifically on tourist railways.

The building of new steam locomotives in China only ceased at the end of the 1980s.

Long live steam

In 1990, there were 7,000 steam, 4,700 diesel, and 1,200 electric locomotives in China. Steam trains were finally withdrawn from use in China in 2003.

Preserved locomotive of Fort Worth & Western Railroad

Preserved steam

The USA was quick to turn from steam power to electric and diesel power. There are, however, a large number of steam locomotives restored to working order in the USA. Train enthusiasts can ride on some of the classic routes, or visit private steam centres.

Veteran locomotives

Although India and Pakistan no longer use steam locomotives, there are still a few tourist steam trains in operation. Locomotives, such as this old British tank engine, attract enthusiasts from all over the world.

53

All decked out

Elaborate decoration took hold in the 19th century. Striking displays promoted the services offered by railway companies, and colourful signs were placed on tunnel entrances to reassure people unfamiliar with rail travel. As competition grew between railway companies, decorations bearing the name of each company appeared on railway property. Huge, colourful cast-iron plaques were hung on railway bridges, and company initials could even be found on the heads of copper nails for slate tiles.

Coat of arms
This Midland Railway coat of arms featured a winged monster and emblems of the cities served by the railway.

TGV nameplate
Many of the French TGV trains' power car units are named after cities served by these trains.

Express train headboard
The headboard displayed the name of the train. It was fastened to the chimney of the locomotive that pulled the train.

American works plate

Works plate
The works plate carries a locomotive's number and date, and often the name and the location of the building company. This plate also bears the name of the company's president.

Lion crest
This crest was displayed on British Railways locomotives and carriages during the 1950s.

Unique trains
Locomotives pulling special trains often carried badges created just for the occasion.

Southern Railway nameplate

Famous names
The names given to locomotives ranged from classical and famous figures to railway directors and names of places served by the railway.

DOMINION OF NEW ZEALAND

London and North Eastern Railway nameplate

Brass nameplate
This brass nameplate commemorated links with the British Commonwealth.

KNIGHT OF · THE GOLDEN FLEECE

Knight of the Golden Fleece
This classical name was carried by an express locomotive of the Great Western Railway.

The crown indicates that the railway was the only one in Canada operated with a Royal Charter.

The headboard carried the name of the service.

DOMINION ATLANTIC RAILWAY. **39**

ATLANTIC COAST EXPRESS

Gold Coast railway
The coat of arms of the Gold Coast Railway featured an elephant, a familiar sight in the country now known as Ghana.

Number plate
This brass number plate is from a 1902 locomotive belonging to the Canadian Dominion Atlantic Railway.

What goes where?
The headboard and nameplate were carried on the locomotive. The railway company's coat of arms was displayed on the locomotive and on the carriages.

Good publicity
Locomotives were usually named after towns and cities served by the railway, as seen on this nameplate of the London Midland and Scottish Railway.

CITY OF MANCHESTER

Local wildlife
A black swan was the symbol of the Western Australian Government Railways from 1890 to 1976.

Scottish flag

English flag

The Caledonian
The shields on this headboard carry motifs of the English and Scottish flags.

THE CALEDONIAN

Travelling underground

Luxury for all

The first underground railway in Moscow opened in 1933. Its stations were famed for their luxurious decor.

The success of the railways in bringing people to large cities also caused problems such as road congestion. In London, UK, this led to the world's first underground railway in 1863, built by digging a trench and then covering it to form a tunnel. Despite the smoky atmosphere, it was quicker and easier than road travel. Later, deeper tunnels were built, and electric trains, lifts, and escalators were introduced. The system became known as the "tube". Over time, other cities around the world began to develop their own electric underground railways.

Early days

Early paintings of the first underground railway show wide tunnels, with natural light filtering through. In reality, the smoke and fumes made travelling on the underground dirty and unpleasant.

All packed in

Underground carriages have automatic sliding doors and wide gangways to provide as much space as possible for commuters, both seated and standing.

Metropolitan Railway Tank Locomotive

This classic underground steam locomotive was built for the Metropolitan Railway in London in 1866. To reduce smoke and steam in the tunnels, the locomotive was fitted with a valve to divert smoke and steam into its water tanks. Unfortunately, this slowed it down. To make up time, drivers did not always operate the valve in the tunnels. Conditions could become unpleasant, especially during rush hours.

The train driver stood here.

Water tank

METROPOLITAN 23 RAILWAY.

The Metro Man

Indian engineer E Sreedharan oversaw the construction and initial operation of the Delhi Metro for 16 years from 1995 until his retirement in 2011. This was a very challenging undertaking, but he simply said, "I refused to give in" and successfully completed the project.

Uniform badge

Railway staff were easily recognized by the striking badges worn as part of their uniform.

London Transport badge with heraldic griffins, from early 1930s

Paris Metro

The underground railway opened in Paris in 1900, and was called the *Metro*. *Metro* stations are very close together and easily recognizable by their signs. Any point in the city centre is within comfortable walking distance of a station.

Reading the map

The Paris *Metro* map relates the route of the train lines to the streets above them. This London Underground map of 1927 is roughly based on a geographical map of London. Maps used today make no attempt to do this, and are not to scale.

Where are we?

Japan's underground railway, which opened in Tokyo in 1927, is extremely large and busy. This Tokyo subway ticket has a route map on one side.

Pipe leading steam and smoke to water tanks

Destination headboard

Automated trains

Most modern rapid transit systems, such as the Metro in Washington D.C. (above), are ideal for automation. Over the past few years, several countries, including India and France, have introduced driverless trains on their underground rail networks.

New York's elevated railway

As street congestion in cities grew, elevated railways were seen as a cheaper and more flexible alternative to underground railways. This elevated railway was built in New York, USA, in the 1880s.

Up in the air

Some railways hang under rails fixed to overhead structures. These can be of two types: suspended, where the train hangs under a rail or rails, and "straddle", where the train fits over a single rail. Suspended trains have wheels that fit onto the rails so there is no risk of trains falling to the ground. Overhead systems with a single rail are called monorails. Modern overhead railways are cheaper to build, offer a good view, and avoid conflict with road traffic. However, they are often noisier than street trains due to their elevated position.

Montmartre funicular

Funicular railways are a type of cable railway, used to carry freight up and down slopes. They were originally built with a double track to balance the system so that loaded wagons travelling down one line helped to pull up empty wagons on the other line. Most funiculars are now electric and carry passengers. This funicular in Montmartre, Paris, was built in 1900, and still operates today.

Out of the way

Monorails, such as this one at the National Motor Museum in England, are often used to transport visitors around exhibitions. Because they are elevated, these railways can cover ground crowded with pedestrians without causing any obstruction.

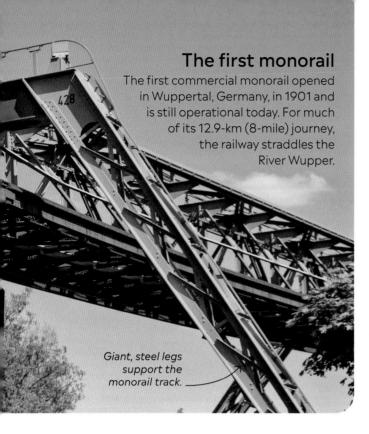

The first monorail

The first commercial monorail opened in Wuppertal, Germany, in 1901 and is still operational today. For much of its 12.9-km (8-mile) journey, the railway straddles the River Wupper.

Giant, steel legs support the monorail track.

👁 **EYEWITNESS**

Eugen Langen
German engineer Eugen Langen (1833–95) developed an overhead electric railway system that included "one-rail" in the title. This led to the use of the word "monorail" for this type of railway. His system was chosen for the city of Wuppertal.

Novelty value

Monorails have great novelty value and are often seen in leisure parks. This open-car monorail operates in a Dutch zoo, where animals may be viewed and photographed in complete safety.

Monorail exhibited in Brisbane, Australia, at the Expo '88 fair

Glasgow rail plane

This rail plane was developed in the 1920s by George Bennie and tried out near Glasgow in Scotland. It was a suspended monorail that travelled along the track using a propeller similar to those used on aeroplanes. However, despite interest from around the world, the rail plane did not progress beyond the experimental stage.

Train with one rail

In most modern monorails, the train straddles the supporting structure. It is balanced and guided by side panels that contain guide wheels. The train runs on electric power, collected from conductor strips set in the side webs of the rail.

Brake van　　　　Milk van　　　　Tanker wagon　　　　Cement wagon

Trains **for fun**

No sooner had railways been invented for transport than people began to build them for amusement. These ranged from simple toy trains for children to push along the floor to complex scale models of full-size trains. The earliest toy trains, made of flat pieces of lead, were followed by wooden trains with rotating wheels. These wooden models were replaced by tin-plate trains running on model tracks, driven at first by clockwork and later by electricity. Over time, enthusiasts began to make and collect miniature scale models of full-size trains.

Smaller than life

Miniature railways are built just for entertainment. They have been popular since the 19th century, especially when pulled by steam.

These images are cut out and made into three-dimensional locomotives.

Cut and paste

Miniature cardboard cutout models are an alternative and cheaper way of collecting models of famous locomotives.

Grand junction railway locomotive

This model of a classic freight locomotive dates from 1846. It has all the features of a full-size train in working order – such as oil lamps, levers, and whistles.

1930s freight train set

Tin-plate trains

British tin-plate clockwork train sets were well-made and built to last. Such sets included lengths of track and other accessories, such as points and tunnels.

Thomas the Tank Engine

Paintings and photographs of railway scenes are often used for jigsaw puzzles. This puzzle features Thomas the Tank Engine, the main character in a popular series of children's books written by the Reverend Awdry in the 1940s.

Board games

The railways appeared in many aspects of everyday life. They even featured in family games, such as this French board game of the 1870s.

Precision-made model

Models are often made of famous locomotives, such as this detailed model of a heavy freight steam locomotive built in the early 1940s for America's Union Pacific Railroad.

Scaled to size

Accurate working scale models are usually made as a hobby by skilled craftspeople. This model, *Lady of Lynn*, is of an express locomotive that ran on the Great Western Railway in Britain in 1908.

The perfect present

Whether simple toys or miniature models, trains still fascinate children and adults alike. Train sets have always made ideal gifts for children. A basic train set can be built up to include stations, bridges, tunnels, signals, and all the elements of a modern railway.

Into the future

New trains and track are constantly being developed, using new materials and more environmentally friendly power sources such as hydrogen. In some cities, electric rapid transit systems have been built using driverless trains that run on rubber tyres along a concrete track. Some countries have developed faster trains to run on existing lines. New lines are also being built. As they produce less pollution than road traffic, and can carry larger cargoes, trains are believed to be the best form of transport for the future.

Driverless trains

Light rail transit systems, such as the Docklands Light Railway in London, UK (above), provide a regular service in congested city centres. The driverless electric trains are controlled by a central computer system.

Freight trains carry anything from cars, to fuel, or sheep.

A freight train removes on average 76 lorries and trucks from the roads.

Magnetic levitation

Maglev is short for magnetic levitation. Instead of travelling on wheels on a rail, the train hovers up to 15 mm (0.59 in) above a metal track, and is pulled along by magnets. This system's many advantages include having no moving parts to wear out, little maintenance, and very quiet trains.

Shanghai Maglev at the Shanghai Pudong International Airport, China

Taking the bend

Tilting trains developed by the Italian Railways are designed to run on high-speed services on upgraded traditional lines. When a curve is detected by the sensor controls, the train is tilted by a hydraulic mechanism to ensure passenger comfort as it goes through the curve.

Pendolino train tilting as it rounds a bend on the West Coast Main Line in the UK.

Tried and failed

The first gas turbine locomotive was built for Swiss Railways in 1941. This picture shows a Canadian National Railway gas turbine-powered train. Like many trains of its kind, it proved to be unreliable, and was withdrawn from service in the 1980s.

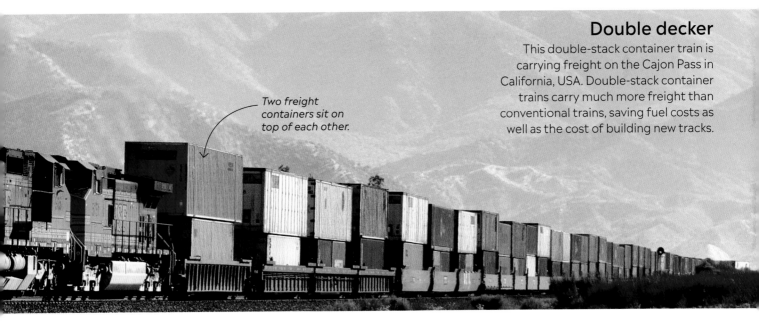

Two freight containers sit on top of each other.

Double decker

This double-stack container train is carrying freight on the Cajon Pass in California, USA. Double-stack container trains carry much more freight than conventional trains, saving fuel costs as well as the cost of building new tracks.

Super train

When the Channel Tunnel opened in 1994, trains ran from Waterloo, London, UK. In 2007, a new terminus opened at London St Pancras International. Eurostar electric train services currently run from London to Paris, France, in 2 hours 15 minutes and from London to Brussels, Belgium, in under two hours.

Green trains

The climate crisis has seen train builders seek new forms of power to drive rolling stock and find an alternative to diesel for heavy freight. In 2019, the UK launched its first hydrogen-powered train HydroFlex in an effort towards reducing carbon emissions.

Great train journeys

There are more than 1.3 million km (800,000 miles) of track on Earth, and each year people travel over 2,200 billion km (1,367 billion miles) by rail, riding everything from Japan's bullet trains to Africa's luxurious *Blue Train*. For extreme tastes, there's the world's steepest rail climb up Ecuador's Devil's Nose Mountain.

The Canadian (Canada)

Travelling 4,466 km (2,775 miles) from Vancouver to Toronto, it passes through the wilderness of the Rockies, the great plains, and the Ontario lakelands.

California *Zephyr* (USA)

Running from San Francisco to Chicago, the California *Zephyr*'s 3,924-km (2,438-mile) route offers dramatic views of the Sierra Nevada Mountains and the upper Colorado River Valley.

Copper Canyon Railway (Mexico)

This 650-km (390-mile) route runs from Los Mochis, near the Pacific coast, to Chihuahua, taking in breathtaking terrain.

Oslo to Bergen (Norway)

NORTH AMERICA

The Canadian

California Zephyr

Coast Starlight: Los Angeles to Seattle (USA)

Durango and Silverton Railway (USA)

Copper Canyon Railway

Havana to Santiago (Cuba)

Road to the Isles: Fort William to Mallaig (Scotland)

Orient Express: London to Istanbul (Trans-Europe)

El Transcantábrico: Santiago de Compostela to Léon (Spain)

Glacier Express

Panama Canal Railway: Colón to Panama City (Panama)

The Devil's Nose: Riobamba to Sibambe (Ecuador)

Lima to Huancayo (Peru)

Cusco to Machu Picchu

Oruro to Tupiza (Bolivia)

Iron-ore desert train: Nouadhibou to Choum (Mauritania)

Dakar to Bamako (Senegal/Mali)

SOUTH AMERICA

Belo Horizonte to Vitoria (Brazil)

Curitiba to Paranaguá (Brazil)

Cusco to Machu Picchu (Peru)

This 112-km (70-mile) ride to Machu Picchu's ancient Inca ruins offers awe-inspiring views of the dramatic canyon along the Urubamba River.

Glacier Express (Switzerland)

Reputed to be the world's slowest express, this train travels 291 km (180 miles) from Zermatt to St Moritz, negotiating 291 bridges and 91 tunnels on the way.

Trans-Siberian Railway (Russia)

Travelling some 9,288 km (5,771 miles) through seven time zones, this is the world's longest rail journey. It runs from Moscow in the west to Vladivostok in the east.

Qingzang railway (China)

This 1,956-km (1,215-mile) route from Lhasa, Tibet, to Xining, Qinghai Province, includes the world's highest section of track through the Tanggula Pass at 5,072 m (16,640 ft).

Trans-Siberian Railway

EUROPE

ASIA

Osaka to Tokyo Shinkansen

Qingzang Railway

Cairo to Aswan (Egypt)

Darjeeling Himalayan Railway: New Jalpaiguri to Darjeeling (India)

Deccan Queen: Mumbai to Pune (India)

AFRICA

Jakarta to Surabaya (Indonesia)

Nairobi to Mombasa (Kenya)

Bangkok to Singapore (Southeast Asia)

Indian Pacific: Perth to Sydney (Australia)

The Ghan

Tranzalpine: Greymouth to Christchurch (New Zealand)

Overlander: Adelaide to Melbourne (Australia)

Blue Train

AUSTRALASIA

Osaka to Tokyo Shinkansen (Japan)

The Osaka–Tokyo Shinkansen was the world's first high-speed train service. Today, the new, ultra-modern Nozomi bullet trains complete the 525-km (325-mile) route, which passes Mount Fuji, in just two-and-a-half hours, reaching speeds of around 300 kph (185 mph).

Blue Train (South Africa)

Running 1,600 km (994 miles) from Cape Town to Pretoria, this luxurious ride offers a butler service and full-size baths.

The Ghan (Australia)

The name refers to the Afghan camel trains that once trekked the same route. It takes 48 hours to travel 2,979 km (1,850 miles) from Darwin to Adelaide.

Train timeline

Around 200 years ago, railways began to revolutionize our world, opening up new opportunities for travel and trade. This new means of transport could carry people and goods faster and further than ever before. This timeline lists some important "firsts" in the history of trains and railways.

1604 A track-way carrying horse-drawn coal wagons on wooden rails is built near Nottingham, UK.

1767 The world's first iron rails for coal wagons are made at Coalbrookedale Iron Works, in Shropshire, UK.

1769 In Paris, France, Nicolas Cugnot builds and demonstrates a steam-powered road carriage – the first-ever self-propelled vehicle.

Flywheel to even out the power

Trevithick's locomotive, 1804

1804 English engineer Richard Trevithick builds the world's first steam locomotive.

1812 The coal-carrying Middleton Railway in Leeds, UK, is the first commercial railway to successfully use steam locomotives.

1825 The Stockton and Darlington Railway in County Durham, UK, is the first public steam railway.

1828 The USA's Delaware & Hudson Railroad is the first operational railway in North America.

1829 George and Robert Stephenson's *Rocket* wins the Rainhill Trials near Liverpool, UK.

1830 The UK's Liverpool & Manchester Railway runs the first scheduled steam passenger services.

1830 *The Best Friend of Charleston* is the first all-American-built locomotive.

1843 The steamship *Great Britain* combines with the express trains of the Great Western Railway to link London, UK, with New York City, USA.

1853 The first railway in India begins operating, connecting the cities of Bombay (now Mumbai) and Thane.

1854 Australia's first railway links Port Melbourne with Melbourne, New South Wales.

1856 In southeastern USA, a railway bridge is built over the Mississippi River for the first time.

The Golden Spike Ceremony at the opening of the US Transcontinental Railroad, 1869

1860 The *Flying Scotsman* begins running between London and Edinburgh, UK.

1863 The world's first underground railway opens in London, UK. It is steam-powered.

1863 The first railway is built in New Zealand.

1869 The Transcontinental Railroad spans North America from east to west.

1871 New York's Grand Central Station opens. It is the world's largest railway station.

1881 The world's first public electric railway opens in Germany.

1885 The Canadian Pacific Railroad begins operating.

1890 An electric underground railway opens in London, UK – it is the first of its kind in the world.

1893 The world's first electric overhead railway opens in Liverpool, UK.

1895 The Baltimore & Ohio Railroad, USA, is the first main line railway to be electrified in the world.

1904 The Trans-Siberian Railway opens from Moscow to Vladivostok, Russia.

1904 The New York City Subway opens.

1913 The world's first regular diesel-train service begins in Sweden.

1928 The UK's *Flying Scotsman* service runs non-stop between London and Edinburgh, covering the 632-km (393-mile) route in 8 hours 3 minutes.

1932 Germany's diesel-powered "Flying Hamburger", the first purpose-built high-speed train, begins running between Hamburg and Berlin.

1932 The LMS railway's new shunting locomotives are the first diesels on the UK rail network.

Cross-section model of the Channel Tunnel, which opened in 1994.

Air duct

Running tunnel

Tunnel for service vehicles

Cross passages link tunnels

1934 Streamlined diesel trains begin running between Los Angeles and New York City.

1934 French railway ETAT introduces a 159-kph (99-mph), lightweight, streamlined petrol railcar.

1935 The *Hiawatha* connecting Chicago with Minneapolis/St Paul, USA, is the fastest scheduled steam service in the world.

1935 A world speed record for non-streamlined steam locomotives of 173 kph (108 mph) is set by the UK's LNER A3 locomotive *Papyrus*.

Moscow subway

1935 The Moscow subway opens its first line.

1938 In the UK, the locomotive *Mallard* sets a world record for steam traction of 203 kph (126 mph).

1941 The USA's Union Pacific Railroad unveils its new locomotive, the 4-8-8-4 Big Boy. It is the largest steam locomotive ever built.

1945 The New York Central Railroad reduces the journey time for the 1,493-km (928-mile) New York–Chicago trip to 16 hours.

1960 Container trains begin operating in the USA.

1964 Japan opens the world's first purpose-built high-speed passenger railway – the bullet train. The line speed is 210 kph (130 mph).

1968 Steam power ends on the UK rail network.

1969 Australia opens the east–west transcontinental rail route from Sydney to Perth.

1970 In America, Penn Central Railway goes bankrupt – the largest corporate failure in US history.

1971 The US government forms AMTRAK to operate all passenger rail services in the USA.

1981 France opens its first TGV high-speed line between Paris and Lyon. It has a top speed of 300 kph (186 mph).

1984 The first double-stack container trains begin operating in the USA.

1984 The world's first maglev train opens at Birmingham International Airport in the UK.

1985 British Rail's High-Speed Train sets a new record for diesel traction of 238 kph (147 mph).

1991 Germany opens its first ICE high-speed rail line.

1994 The Channel Tunnel opens, providing an undersea rail link between the UK and France.

2001 In Australia, the world's longest ever train measures 7.3 km (4.5 miles). It consists of 682 cars and eight locomotives.

Japan's N700 bullet train, 2007

2003 Japan's experimental maglev train sets a new world speed record of 581 kph (361 mph).

2004 China opens the Shanghai maglev line. Trains can reach 350 kph (220 mph) in two minutes.

2006 China opens the world's highest railway, linking Beijing with Lhasa in Tibet, via Xining.

2006 The USA's Union Pacific Railroad sets a world record of 172 million tonnes of coal moved in one year.

2007 A specially designed French V150 TGV sets a new world record for electric traction of 574 kph (356 mph).

2007 Japan unveils its new N700 "green" bullet train, which delivers high-speed rail services with reduced energy use.

2018 First hydrogen-powered train enters service in northern Germany.

2020 China launches the first driverless bullet train, which runs between Beijing and Zhangjiakou, with a top speed of 350 kph (217 mph).

Find out more

Because trains are so popular, there is a wealth of places to go to discover more about railways. You can ride historic trains on a heritage railway or visit transport museums to see railway artefacts. Your local library is likely to have railway books, and you can search the internet for rail enthusiast groups, events, and special trains.

Goathland Station, North Yorkshire Moors Railway, UK

Heritage railways

Around the world there are many heritage railways where you can still ride on steam trains and sometimes even get a lesson in how to drive a steam locomotive.

USEFUL WEBSITES

• Wikipedia has many articles about railways, famous trains, and railway history: **http://en.wikipedia.org/wiki/History_of_rail_transport**
• Find out how locomotives, maglevs, and other rail technology works at How Stuff Works: **www.howstuffworks.com**
• The UK's National Railway Museum has online exhibitions, photo galleries, movie clips, and audio recordings: **www.railwaymuseum.org.uk**
• The UK Heritage Railways site has technical details about locomotives, carriages, and signalling systems: **www.heritagerailways.com**
• Trainweb is an amazing US site for all things train-related, from trips to videos: **www.trainweb.com**
• The National Railroad Museum of America tells the story of how rail shaped the USA: **www.nationalrrmuseum.org**
• The National Railway Historical Society is the main US umbrella group for all rail fans: **www.nrhs.com**
• The website of the National Railway Museum in Port Adelaide, Australia, has online photo exhibitions of locomotives, carriages, railcars, and stations: **www.natrailmuseum.org.au**
• For details of how to travel by rail anywhere in the world, see: **www.seat61.com**

Museum visits

Transport museums usually have sections devoted to trains, and most countries have a dedicated national railway museum. These are great places to get an overview of the development of trains and railway technology.

A steam locomotive at the Swiss Museum of Transport, Lucerne, Switzerland.

Velorail in Brittany, France

Riding the rails

In some places, old disused railway tracks have been turned into paths, allowing you to follow the routes once travelled by locomotives. In France, Sweden, Germany, and some other parts of Europe there are also velorails. Here you can pedal your own "carriage" over sections of preserved track no longer used by trains.

TRAINS IN THE MOVIES

Harry Potter films (2001–2011)
In these films about a young wizard, a steam train called the Hogwarts Express takes Harry and his pals to wizard school. Hogwarts station is really Goathland (see opposite) on the North Yorkshire Moors Railway.

The Polar Express (2004)
A magical train pulls up at a boy's house on the night before Christmas and invites him to travel to the North Pole to meet Santa.

The Railway Children (1970)
Based on Edith Nesbit's novel this much-loved film tells the story of children growing up beside a railway track in Victorian England.

Harry Potter and the Chamber of Secrets (2002)

Microsoft® Train Simulator computer game

In the driving seat

A train simulator is a video game that lets you experience what it's like to be in a locomotive's driving seat. This typically involves using the controls in a "virtual" cab to drive the train on a computerized representation of an actual route. More complex versions let you operate signals, and design your own routes.

Snapping and spotting

Famous locomotives often come out on special occasions, giving rail enthusiasts a chance to photograph their favourite engines. "Train spotting" (collecting the numbers of engines still in service), is also a popular hobby among rail fans.

PLACES TO VISIT

Baltimore & Ohio Railroad Museum, Baltimore, Maryland, USA
The most comprehensive US collection of railway exhibits.

Cité du Train, Mulhouse, France
The world-renowned French National Railway Museum houses many classic French locomotives.

National Railroad Museum, Green Bay, Wisconsin, USA
Over 70 locomotives and rail cars, including *Big Boy* – the largest locomotive ever.

National Railway Museum, York, UK
The world's largest collection of trains and railway artefacts, including Stephenson's original *Rocket* locomotive.

North Yorkshire Moors Railway, UK
The UK's most popular heritage steam railway runs through beautiful moorland.

Science Museum, London, UK
Includes lots of exhibits on railways, including *Puffing Billy* (1813).

State Railroad Museum, Sacramento, California, USA
This tells the story of California's railroads and their impact on the "golden state".

Glossary

AIR BRAKE A brake that relies on controlling air pressure to apply and release the brake.

BELL CODE A language for describing trains used by signallers to despatch and receive trains.

BELL TAPPER A device used to tap out bell signals between signallers.

BLOCK A section of railway controlled by a specific signaller or signal tower.

BOGIE A wheeled chassis or framework that is attached to a locomotive or railway carriage by a swivel mounting.

BRAKE VAN A rail vehicle that provides braking power for goods trains and accommodation for the train guard.

BUFFER A shock absorber between rail vehicles.

BULLHEAD RAIL A type of rail developed in the UK, where the top half of the rail mirrors the bottom half. Once the running side was worn out, the rail was turned over and reused.

CAB The part of a locomotive from which the driver controls the train.

CARRIAGE A passenger vehicle on a train, also called a car (especially in North America).

CAST IRON A form of iron that can be cast, or moulded, into almost any shape when molten. Cast iron was used to make rails and bridges in the early days of railways. It was later replaced by stronger wrought iron.

Cast-iron emblem on a London railway bridge

CHIMNEY The outlet on a steam locomotive, through which the gases from the coal fire escape into the air.

CONTAINER A metal freight box that can be packed with goods and then transported by ships, trains, and trucks.

COUPLING The method of connecting rail vehicles together.

CRANK Part of a steam locomotive that transmits power from the piston to the driving wheels.

CUTTING A large ditch cut through the landscape to provide a more level route.

CYLINDER A chamber in an engine in which steam expands or fuel ignites to push pistons back and forth, and so generate power.

DIESEL LOCOMOTIVE A locomotive powered by a diesel engine.

DIESEL-ELECTRIC LOCOMOTIVE A locomotive with a diesel engine that produces power for electric traction motors, which drive the wheels.

DRIVING WHEEL A wheel that propels a locomotive along a track. On a steam locomotive, the driving wheels are powered by the pistons. On diesel and electric locomotives, electric motors supply power to the driving wheels.

ELECTRIC TRAIN A train that uses electricity from an external source – such as an overhead power line, third rail, or on-board batteries – to power traction motors on the train.

ELEVATED RAILWAY A railway built on raised platforms through city streets, such as the former Liverpool Overhead Railway in the UK and part of the New York Subway, USA.

EMBANKMENT An earthen structure designed to raise a railway above the natural ground level.

EXHAUST PIPE The pipe that allows waste gases from a diesel engine to escape.

FIREBOX A metal box in the heart of a steam locomotive, in which the fire is kept.

Diesel locomotive

FIRE TUBE The fire tube conveys heat from a steam locomotive's fire to the boiler. This boils the water and makes steam.

FISH-BELLY RAIL A type of early cast-iron rail with a curved underside.

FLANGED WHEEL A railway wheel with a metal lip called a flange on the inside edge.

FLAT-BOTTOMED RAIL The standard rail of today, which takes the form of a T-shape with a wide, flat base.

FREIGHT A term used to describe trains transporting finished goods and raw materials. It can also refer to the load itself.

FUNICULAR RAILWAY Used on tram, cliff, and industrial lines, funicular railways use cables or chains to pull vehicles up and down slopes.

Funicular railway in Pau, France

GAUGE The measurement between the rails of a track. The world's most common gauge is 1,435 mm (4 ft 8.5 in), and is known as standard gauge.

GAUGE GLASSES A device on a steam locomotive that shows the driver the level of water in the boiler. If the boiler were to run dry, the locomotive would explode.

HEADBOARD A notice on the front of a train that gives the train's name, route, or destination.

LEVEL CROSSING A place where a road crosses a railway track on flat ground.

LOCOMOTIVE A self-propelled railway vehicle that can haul a train. There are steam, diesel, and electric locomotives.

MAGLEV TRAIN A train that works by being suspended and propelled over special tracks by electromagnetic force. Maglevs produce virtually no friction, and are very quiet.

MONORAIL A train that runs on a single rail.

OFF A signal is "off" when it is indicating that a train can proceed.

PISTON Part of a steam locomotive that drives the wheels. It consists of a rod inside a cylinder that is pushed in and out by steam. Other rods harness this motion and turn the wheels.

PLATE RAIL L-shaped iron rails used on plateways to guide wagons with plain wheels. (Railway vehicles today have flanged wheels.)

PLATEWAY An early railway that used plate rail, often built as a feeder line to a canal or river.

POINTS Pieces of track that allow a train to switch from one set of tracks to another.

PULLMAN CAR A luxury railway carriage for those who can pay a higher fare. Pullmans were introduced in the USA in 1865 as sleeping cars on long-distance trains, but the name later became synonymous with high-class rail travel.

RACK RAILWAY A railway with an additional toothed rack-rail. The train or locomotive is fitted with a cog that links with the teeth on the rack-rail, enabling it to climb very steep slopes.

RAILCAR A self-propelled passenger vehicle, usually with the engine located under the floor.

RAILWAY TIME Different places in the same country often had their own local time. In the 1840s, railways began to introduce a standardized "railway time" to avoid confusion caused by local time differences.

Rack railway in Snowdonia, Wales

SHUNTER A small locomotive for moving trucks or wagons around a marshalling yard.

SIGNAL A fixed unit with an arm or a light that indicates whether a train should stop, go, or slow down. A signal also starts a train, whether it is by a whistle, hand gesture, or bell code.

SIGNAL BOX/SIGNAL TOWER A building in which the movement of trains is controlled by use of signals and coded messages sent from one signal box or tower to another.

Monorail at Walt Disney World, Florida, USA

SLEEPER The cross-piece supporting the rails of a track, made out of wood, concrete, or steel.

SLEEPING CAR A carriage with beds where passengers can sleep while travelling. Sleeping cars were first used in the USA in the 1830s.

STEAM LOCOMOTIVE A locomotive that generates steam by boiling water. The steam is then fed to cylinders that drive the wheels.

TAILLIGHT The lamp at the rear of a train. In the UK, a train is not complete without an illuminated rear warning light.

TANK ENGINE A steam engine that carries the water and coal it uses on the locomotive itself, rather than towing it behind in a tender.

TENDER The truck or wagon behind a steam locomotive that holds the locomotive's fuel and water.

TILTING TRAIN A train that can lean into bends, enabling it to travel faster along a route with many curves.

Loading rail trucks in Ghana

TOOTHED RAIL An additional rail often used on mountain railways to enable a train to climb a steep hill (see Rack railway).

TRAILING WHEEL An unpowered wheel located behind the driving wheels of a steam locomotive that provides support.

TRAIN An assembly of power unit and wagons or carriages running on rails, carrying freight or passengers. If it is just the power unit, then it is a locomotive.

TRAIN FERRIES Ferries designed to take rail vehicles by having a deck with tracks.

TRUCK A small rail wagon.

VACUUM BRAKE A type of brake that is held off by a partial vacuum, and applied when air is let into the system.

WAGON A rail vehicle for carrying freight.

WROUGHT IRON A form of iron that is worked by being forged or hammered, and which was used before the invention of steel.

Index

Acknowledgments

The publisher would like to thank the following people for their help with making the book: Staff at the National Railway Museum, York, especially David Wright and Richard Gibbon; John Liffen at the Science Museum; Justin Scobie for photographic assistance; The London Transport Museum; the signal box staff of Three Bridges (British Rail) Station, West Sussex; The Bluebell Railway; Gatwick Airport; Robert Gwynne and Russell Hollowood at the National Rail Museum, York, for assisting with updates; Claire Gillard for initial research; Rupa Rao, Helena Spiteri, Lisa Stock, and Gin von Noorden for editorial assistance; Earl Neish for design assistance; Sue Nicholson and Edward Kinsey for the wallchart; Vijay Kandwal for colour work; Priyanka Sharma-Saddi for the jacket; Ann Baggaley for proofreading; and Elizabeth Wise for the index.

The publisher would like to thank the following for their kind permission to reproduce their photographs:
(Key: a-above; b-below/bottom; c-centre; f-far; l-left; r-right; t-top)
Advertising Archives: 26bc; **Alamy Images:** 33tc, Artepics Bridgeman Images 30cb, Anthony Brown 49ca, Bradley Caslin 47cla, Historic Collection 29tc, Jerry Tavin / Everett Collection 25tr, The Print Collector 8tr, Alex Fairweather 7cra, FineArt 13cra, ILYA GENKIN 23bc, Dennis Schmelz / Mauritius images GmbH 43l, Paul Heinrich 52-53c, Science History Images 41tr, World History Archive 42bc, imageBROKER 58-59tl, J3BJP4 59tr, Niday Picture Library 36tl, Ben McRae 47tr, Granger, NYC 19crb, Granger, NYC. 39tr, eye35.pix 49br, Dave Porter 6-7t, Qaphotos.com 21clb, Christoph Rueegg 41cr, Steve Tulley 63bl, Asar Studios 11ca, Daniel Wyre 53tc, Zoonar / zhang zhiwei 33b; Steve Crise / Transtock Inc. 62-63c; Michael Grant 70lb; JTB Photo Communications, Inc. 65bl, 65tl; James Lovell 68tr; Iain Masterton 67br; Sami Sarkis France 69tl; Nick Suydam 64cla. **alimdi.net:** Photographers Direct 68br. **Aquarius Library:** Warner Bros 69tr. **Australian Overseas Information Service, London:** 42tr. **Barlow Reid:** 41cl. **Bettmann Archive / Hulton Picture Library:** 19t. **Bridgman Art Library / Science**

Museum, London: 11btc; National Railway Museum, York 11tr; Private Collections: 13btc; Guildhall Library, Corporation of London: 56cl. **Bridgeman Images:** Peter Newark American Pictures 18tl. **Britt Allcroft (Thomas Ltd), 1989:** 61tr. **Jean-Loup Charmet:** 10cra, 30bl, 39bl, 44cl, 56tr. **J.A. Coiley:** 54cr, 58br. **Corbis:** Eleanor Bentall 65br; Ursula Gahwiler / Robert Harding World Imagery 64tr; Colin Garratt, Milepost 92 _ 71cr; Gavin Hellier / Robert Harding World Imagery 67cl; Dave G. Houser 64bc; Bruno Morandi / Robert Harding World Imagery 65tc; Michael Reynolds / EPA 65tr; Phil Schermeister 64bl; Naoaki Watanabe / amanaimages 65cr; Culver Pictures Inc.: 11tl, 16btr, 19br, 37tl, 41btr. **DK Images:** Rough Guides 71ct, 71bl. **Docklands Light Railway Ltd / Marysha Alwan:** 62tl. **drr.net:** Joern Sackermann 69bc. **e.t. archive:** 6bl, 9cl, 9tc, 9c, 12cra, 16bl, 20tr, 26btr (detail); 28cr, 29ca, 32tr, 46cl, 49bca, 51tr. **Getty Images:** Construction Photography / Avalon 46-47b, Bettmann 20cb, Franck Chazot 58clb, Print Collector 21cra, Mike Danneman 26-27t, FatCamera 61b, Science & Society Picture Library 9tc, Science & Society Picture Library 15tc, Science & Society Picture Library Bridgeman Images 12-13b, Prakash Singh 57tc, Paolo Vieceli 35clb; Hulton Archive / Andrew Joseph Russell / MPI 66br. **Getty Images / iStock:** ZU_09 42cl. **Hulton Picture Company:** 31btl. **Hutchison Picture Library:** 53acr. **Antony J. Lambert:** 45c, 60car. **La vie du rail, Paris:** 39ca, 39tl. **Mack Sennet Productions:** 25acr. **Mansell Collection Ltd:** 23. **Mary Evans Picture Library:** 8br, 9cr, 12t, 17btl, 21cr, 28cl, 41tr, 61acl. **John Massey Stewart:** 45bcl, 59cl. **Microsoft:** Microsoft product screen shot reprinted with permission from Microsoft Corporation 69c. **Millbrook House Ltd:** 7abl, 22br, 37br, 51btl, 58acl, 63tr. **National Railway Museum:** 6cl, 6cr, 13btr, 21tr, 22bc, 25cr, 25bcr, 26cr, 30bc, 35cr, 37btr, 43bcr, 49tl, 50cr, 59cr; Terence Cuneo: 33c. **PA Photos:** DPA Deutsche Press-Agentur / DPA 62br. **Peter Newark's Picture Library:** 13cr, 18cr, 19c, 19tr, 24acr, 34tl, 42crb, 43br, 53cr. **Quadrant Picture Library:** 27btc, 43crb, 53crb. **Rank Films:** 49cl. **Retrograph Archive / Martin Breese:** 37cr. **Robert Harding Picture Library:** 52cl,

58bl. **Telegraph Colour Library:** 50tr, 57c. **Weintraub / Ronald Grant:** 31tl. **Zefa Picture Library:** 24tl, 35tl, 59b. **University of Birmingham:** 63br; **Dreamstime.com:** Richie Chan 22-23c. **Science Photo Library:** Maertin Bond 63tl. **University of Pittsburgh:** 35br.

Wallchart: Alamy: cl. **Corbis:** José Fuste Raga / zefa br. **DK Images:** National Railway Museum, York cla (Stephenson's Rocket), clb (diesel locomotive), clb (train tickets), cl (tea set), cl (ticket clippers), cra (wheel), tr (workman's pick); Science Museum, London tl (Trevithick's train). **PA Photos:** DPA Deutsche Press-Agentur / DPA bl (Maglev train). **Photolibrary:** imagebroker cr.

All other images © Dorling Kindersley
For further information see:
www.dkimages.com